TO

My wonderful husband

FROM

Your wonderful wife

Happy First Anniversary
7/7/08

FAMILY
CHRISTIAN
PRESS

GOD'S PROMISES

YOUR MARRIAGE

The quoted ideas expressed in this book (but not scripture verses) are not, in all cases, exact quotations, as some have been edited for clarity and brevity. In all cases, the author has attempted to maintain the speaker's original intent. In some cases, quoted material for this book was obtained from secondary sources, primarily print media. While every effort was made to ensure the accuracy of these sources, the accuracy cannot be guaranteed. For additions, deletions, corrections or clarifications in future editions of this text, please write FAMILY CHRISTIAN PRESS.

Scripture quotations are taken from:

The Holy Bible, King James Version

The Holy Bible, New International Version (NIV) Copyright © 1973, 1978, 1984, by International Bible Society. Used by permission of Zondervan Publishing House. All rights reserved.

The Holy Bible, New King James Version (NKJV) Copyright © 1982 by Thomas Nelson, Inc. Used by permission.

The New American Standard Bible®, (NASB) Copyright © 1960, 1962, 1963, 1968, 1971, 1972, 1973, 1975, 1977, 1995 by The Lockman Foundation. Used by permission.

Holy Bible, New Living Translation, (NLT)copyright © 1996. Used by permission of Tyndale House Publishers, Inc., Wheaton, Illinois 60189. All rights reserved.

The Message (MSG)- This edition issued by contractual arrangement with NavPress, a division of The Navigators, U.S.A. Originally published by NavPress in English as THE MESSAGE: The Bible in Contemporary Language copyright 2002-2003 by Eugene Peterson. All rights reserved.

New Century Version®. (NCV) Copyright © 1987, 1988, 1991 by Word Publishing, a division of Thomas Nelson, Inc. All rights reserved. Used by permission.

The Holman Christian Standard Bible™ (Holman CSB) Copyright © 1999, 2000, 2001 by Holman Bible Publishers. Used by permission.

Cover Design by Kim Russell / Wahoo Designs
Page Layout by Bart Dawson

ISBN 1-58334-333-4

Printed in the United States of America

GOD'S PROMISES

YOUR MARRIAGE

TABLE OF CONTENTS

INTRODUCTION

Now these three remain: faith, hope, and love.
But the greatest of these is love.

1 Corinthians 13:13 Holman CSB

"But the greatest of these is love"—seven familiar words that remind us of a simple truth: God places a high priority on love … and so should we. Faith is important, of course. So, too, is hope. But love is more important still.

This text contains 18 Biblically based principles that can help you and your spouse fashion a loving relationship that will stand the test of time. These common-sense tools can help you build your marriage upon the only foundation that can never be shaken—the foundation of God's Holy Word.

When you use God's Word as the blueprint for your marriage, you'll feel differently about your spouse, you'll feel differently about your family, you'll feel differently about your world, and you'll feel differently about your future.

So make this promise to yourself, to your spouse, and to your God: promise that you will use the ideas on these pages to make your marriage a model of Christian love. Promise, also, that you will seek God's guidance for your marriage, and that you will trust the guidance that He gives. When you do, your Heavenly Father will bless you and your family today, tomorrow, and forever.

So make this promise to yourself and to your Creator: promise that you will use the ideas on these pages to help in your marriage. Promise, also, that you will seek God's guidance for every facet of your life, and that you will trust the guidance that He gives. When you do, the Father will bless you and yours today, tomorrow, and forever.

PUT GOD FIRST

If you love me, you will obey what I command.

John 14:15 NIV

Do you and your spouse put God first in your marriage? Or do you allow yourselves to be hijacked by the inevitable obligations and distractions of 21st-century life? When you and your beloved allow Christ to reign over your lives and your marriage, your household will be eternally blessed.

God loved this world so much that He sent His Son to save it. And now only one real question remains: what will you and yours do in response to God's love? The answer should be obvious: You must put God first in every aspect of your lives, including your marriage.

God is with you always, listening to your thoughts and prayers, watching over your every move. As the demands of everyday life weigh down upon you, you may be tempted to ignore God's presence or—worse yet—to rebel against His commandments. But, when you quiet yourself and acknowledge His presence, God touches your heart and restores your spirits.

At this very moment, God is seeking to work in you and through you. So why not let Him do it right now?

A TIP

Today, think about ways that you can glorify God
by placing Him first in your life.

Faith is obedience at home
and looking to the Master;
obedience is faith going out
to do His will.

Andrew Murray

Promises from God's Word About . . .
GOD FIRST

Jesus said to him, "'You shall love the Lord your God with all your heart, with all your soul, and with all your mind.' This is the first and great commandment."

Matthew 22:37-38 NKJV

We love Him because He first loved us.

1 John 4:19 NKJV

And we know that in all things God works for the good of those who love him, who have been called according to his purpose.

Romans 8:28 NIV

It is good to praise the Lord and make music to your name, O Most High, to proclaim your love in the morning and your faithfulness at night....

Psalm 92:1-2 NIV

If you love me, you will obey what I command.

John 14:15 NIV

More Ideas About . . .
GOD FIRST

All to Jesus I surrender, all to Him I freely give.
I will ever love and trust Him,
in His presence daily give.

Judson W. Van De Venter

True faith commits us to obedience.

A. W. Tozer

The cross that Jesus commands you and me to carry
is the cross of submissive obedience to the will of
God, even when His will includes suffering and
hardship and things we don't want to do.

Anne Graham Lotz

Our obedience does not make God any bigger or
better than He already is. Anything God commands
of us is so that our joy may be full—the joy of
seeing His glory revealed to us and in us!

Beth Moore

Promises from God's Word About . . .
OBEDIENCE

*It is the Lord your God you must follow, and him you
must revere. Keep his commands and obey him;
serve him and hold fast to him.*

Deuteronomy 13:4 NIV

*The world and its desires pass away, but the man who
does the will of God lives forever.*

1 John 2:17 NIV

*Does the Lord delight in burnt offerings and sacrifices as
much as in obeying the voice of the Lord?
To obey is better than sacrifice....*

1 Samuel 15:22 NIV

*Peter and the other apostles replied:
"We must obey God rather than men!"*

Acts 5:29 NIV

More Ideas About . . .
OBEDIENCE

Every day, I find countless opportunities to decide whether I will obey God and demonstrate my love for Him or try to please myself or the world system. God is waiting for my choices.

Bill Bright

Obedience is the natural outcome of belief.

C. H. Spurgeon

God does not want the forced obedience of slaves. Instead, He covets the voluntary love and obedience of children who love Him for Himself.

Catherine Marshall

Obedience is the key of knowledge.

Christina Rossetti

Peter said, "No, Lord!" But he had to learn that one cannot say "No" while saying "Lord" and that one cannot say "Lord" while saying "No."

Corrie ten Boom

A TIP

Obedience to God is not optional;
View obedience as a requirement.

A PRAYER

Dear Lord, Your love is eternal and Your laws are
everlasting. When I obey Your commandments,
I am blessed. Today, I invite You to reign over every
corner of my heart. I will have faith in You, Father.
I will sense Your presence; I will accept Your love;
I will trust Your will; and I will praise You for
the Savior of my life: Your Son Jesus.
Amen

THE POWER OF LOVE

Beloved, if God so loved us,
we also ought to love one another.

1 John 4:11 NASB

The familiar words of 1st Corinthians 13 remind us of the importance and the power of love. Yet sometimes, amid the inevitable struggles of everyday life, we may lose sight—at least temporarily—of the role that love should play in every Christian life and in every Christian marriage.

Christ showed His love for us on the cross, and, as Christians we are called to return Christ's love by sharing it. We are commanded (not advised, not encouraged…commanded!) to love one another just as Christ loved us (John 13:34). That's a tall order, but as Christians, we are obligated to follow it. And as men and women who have been joined together in the eyes of God, we must strive to love our spouses . . . even when our spouses behave in ways that disappoint us or frustrate us.

Sometimes love is easy (puppies and sleeping children come to mind) and sometimes love is hard (imperfect husbands and wives come to mind). But God's Word is clear: We are to love all our family members, friends, and neighbors, not just the ones who seem most lovable. So today, take time to share Christ's love by word and by example. And the greatest of these is, of course, is example.

A TIP

Believe that your treatment toward all members
of your family should be based upon
a foundation of love.

For Jesus, peace seems to have meant
not the absence of struggle
but the presence of love.

Frederick Buechner

Promises from God's Word About . . .
LOVE

Love one another deeply, from the heart.

1 Peter 1:22 NIV

*Above all, love each other deeply, because love covers
over a multitude of sins.*

1 Peter 4:8 NIV

*I pray that you, being rooted and firmly established in
love, may be able to comprehend with all the saints what
is the breadth and width, height and depth, and to know
the Messiah's love that surpasses knowledge,
so you may be filled with all the fullness of God.*

Ephesians 3:17-19 Holman CSB

*Though I speak with the tongues of men and of angels,
but have not love, I have become sounding brass
or a clanging cymbal.*

1 Corinthians 13:1 NKJV

More Ideas About . . .
LOVE

It is important to know that you have to work to
keep love alive; you have to protect it and
maintain it, just like you would a delicate flower.

James Dobson

To love abundantly is to live abundantly,
and to love forever is to live forever.

Henry Drummond

What we have once enjoyed we can never lose.
All whom we love deeply become a part of us.

Helen Keller

You always win a better response with love.

Helen Hosier

Hating people is like burning down your own house
to get rid of a rat.

Harry Emerson Fosdick

Promises from God's Word About . . .
LOVE

Love each other like brothers and sisters. Give each other more honor than you want for yourselves.

Romans 12:10 NCV

I give you a new commandment: that you love one another. Just as I have loved you, you should also love one another. By this all people will know that you are My disciples, if you have love for one another.

John 13:34-35 Holman CSB

And the Lord make you to increase and abound in love one toward another, and toward all men. . . .

1 Thessalonians 3:12 KJV

Now these three remain: faith, hope, and love. But the greatest of these is love.

1 Corinthians 13:13 Holman CSB

More Ideas About . . .
LOVE

We've grown to be one soul—two parts; our lives are
so intertwined that when some passion stirs
your heart, I feel the quake in mine.

Gloria Gaither

A man and woman should choose each other for
life for the simple reason that a long life is barely
enough time for a man and woman to understand
each other, and to understand is to love.

George Truett

Christ made love the stairway that would enable
all Christians to climb to heaven. Hold fast to it,
therefore, in all sincerity, give one another
practical proof of it, and by your progress,
make your ascent together.

Fulgence of Ruspe

Sacrificial love, giving-up love, is love that is
willing to go to any lengths to provide for
the well-being of the beloved.

Ed Young

A TIP

Express Yourself: Since you love your family,
you should tell them so . . . a lot!

A PRAYER

Dear Heavenly Father, You have blessed us with
a love that is infinite and eternal. In response to
Your gifts, let us be loving servants, Father, and
let us demonstrate our faith by placing You first in
our marriage and in every other aspect of our lives.
Amen

THE GOLDEN RULE

*Just as you want others to do for you,
do the same for them.*

Luke 6:31 Holman CSB

Is the Golden Rule one of the rules that governs your household? Hopefully so. Obeying the Golden Rule is a proven way to improve any relationship, including your marriage. But the reverse is also true: if you or your spouse ignore the Golden Rule altogether, you're headed for trouble, and fast.

Too many marriages become unbalanced when one partner assumes the role of the "taker" while the other partner accepts the role of the "giver." But the healthiest marriages are those in which both parties seek to give more than they get.

Jesus made Himself perfectly clear: He instructed us to treat others in the same way that we want to be treated. That means that we must treat other people (including our loved ones) with respect, kindness, and courtesy.

So if you're wondering how you should treat your spouse (or anyone else, for that matter), ask the person you see every time you look into the mirror. The answer you receive will tell you exactly what to do.

A TIP

What's good for you is good for them, too.
If you want others to treat you according to
the Golden Rule, then you should be quick to
treat them in the same way. In other words,
always play by the rule: the Golden Rule.

Show respect for all people.
Love the brothers and sisters of
God's family.

1 Peter 2:17 ICB

Promises from God's Word About . . .
THE GOLDEN RULE

*Let us not become weary in doing good, for at the proper
time we will reap a harvest if we do not give up.*

Galatians 6:9 NIV

*Each of you should look not only to your own interests,
but also to the interest of others.*

Philippians 2:4 NIV

*So in everything, do to others what you would have them
do to you, for this sums up the Law and the Prophets.*

Matthew 7:12 NIV

*Give to everyone who asks you, and if anyone takes
what belongs to you, do not demand it back.*

Luke 6:30 NIV

*Carry each other's burdens, and in this way
you will fulfill the law of Christ.*

Galatians 6:2 NIV

More Ideas About . . .
THE GOLDEN RULE

It is one of the most beautiful compensations of
life that no one can sincerely try to help another
without helping herself.

Barbara Johnson

We should behave to our friends as we would wish
our friends to behave to us.

Aristotle

The Golden Rule starts at home,
but it should never stop there.

Marie T. Freeman

Anything done for another is done for oneself.

Pope John Paul II

It is wrong for anyone to be anxious to receive
more from his neighbor than he himself
is willing to give to God.

St. Francis of Assisi

Promises from God's Word About . . .
KINDNESS

May the Lord cause you to increase and abound
in love for one another, and for all people.

1 Thessalonians 3:12 NASB

And be ye kind one to another, tenderhearted,
forgiving one another, even as God for
Christ's sake hath forgiven you.

Ephesians 4:32 KJV

Verily I say unto you, Inasmuch as ye have done it
unto one of the least of these my brethren,
ye have done it unto me.

Matthew 25:40 KJV

Be ye therefore merciful,
as your Father also is merciful.

Luke 6:36 KJV

More Ideas About . . .
KINDNESS

When you launch an act of kindness out into the crosswinds of life, it will blow kindness back to you.

Dennis Swanberg

Reach out and care for someone who needs the touch of hospitality. The time you spend caring today will be a love gift that will blossom into the fresh joy of God's Spirit in the future.

Emilie Barnes

Let Christ be formed in me, and let me learn of him all lowliness of heart, all gentleness of bearing, all modesty of speech, all helpfulness of action, and promptness in the doing of my Father's will.

John Baillie

The mark of a Christian is that he will walk the second mile and turn the other cheek. A wise man or woman gives the extra effort, all for the glory of the Lord Jesus Christ.

John Maxwell

A TIP

Kindness Every Day: Kindness should be an integral part of your marriage every day, not just on the days when you feel good. And remember: small acts of kindness can make a big difference.

A PRAYER

Lord, sometimes this world can become a place of busyness, frustration, and confusion. Slow me down, Lord, that I might see the needs of those around me. Today, help me show mercy to those in need. Today, let me spread kind words of thanksgiving and celebration in honor of Your Son. Today, let forgiveness rule my heart. And every day, Lord, let my love for Christ be reflected through deeds of kindness for those who need the healing touch of the Master's hand.
Amen

TOTAL COMMITMENT

Wives, understand and support your husbands by submitting to them in ways that honor the Master. Husbands, go all out in love for your wives. Don't take advantage of them.

Colossians 3:18-19 MSG

Sometimes, it's easy to be in love—just ask any blissful young couple who recently got engaged! But sometimes, love isn't quite as easy as that—just ask any long-married couple who faces health problems, financial difficulties, family tragedy, or any other significant brand of trouble. Honest-to-goodness love is strong enough to weather these storms because honest-to-goodness love isn't a feeling that comes and goes; it's a level of commitment that remains steady and strong, even when times are tough.

Every marriage, like every life, will encounter days of hardship and pain. It is during these difficult days that husbands and wives discover precisely what their marriage is made of.

God's Word makes it clear: genuine love is committed love. Genuine love is more than a feeling . . . it is a decision to make love endure, no matter what. So, if you want your love to last forever, then you and your spouse must be totally committed to each other. When you are, then you can rest assured that the two of you—plus God—can handle anything that comes your way.

A TIP

Commitment first! The best marriages are built
upon an unwavering commitment to God and
an unwavering commitment to one's spouse.
So, if you're totally committed, congratulations;
if you're not, you're building your marriage
(and your life) on a very shaky foundation.

Wherever your marriage is today,
make or reaffirm you unyielding
commitment to its permanence.

Ed Young

Promises from God's Word About . . .
MARRIAGE

*Nevertheless let each one of you in particular
so love his own wife as himself, and let the wife see
that she respects her husband.*

Ephesians 5:33 NKJV

*Therefore shall a man leave his father and his mother,
and shall cleave unto his wife:
and they shall be one flesh.*

Genesis 2:24 KJV

*So then, they are no longer two but one flesh.
Therefore what God has joined together,
let not man separate.*

Matthew 19:6 NKJV

Honor marriage, and guard the sacredness of sexual
intimacy between wife and husband. God draws
a firm line against casual and illicit sex.

Hebrews 13:4 MSG

More Ideas About . . .
MARRIAGE

Marital love is a committed act of the will before
it is anything else. It is sacrificial love,
a no-turning-back decision.

Ed Young

So I go to church, not because of any legalistic or
moralistic reasons, but because I am a hungry sheep
who needs to be fed; and for the same reason that
I wear a wedding ring: a public witness of
a private commitment.

Madeleine L'Engle

Those who abandon ship the first time it enters
a storm miss the calm beyond. And the rougher
the storms weathered together, the deeper
and stronger real love grows.

Ruth Bell Graham

Your mate doesn't live by bread alone;
he or she needs to be "buttered" from time to time.

Zig Ziglar

Promises from God's Word About . . .
COMMITMENT

If you do not stand firm in your faith,
you will not stand at all.

Isaiah 7:9 NIV

So prepare your minds for service and have self-control.

1 Peter 1:13 NCV

Apply your heart to discipline and your ears
to words of knowledge.

Proverbs 23:12 NASB

So let's keep focused on that goal [reaching out to
Christ], those of us who want everything God has for
us. If any of you have something else in mind, something
less than total commitment, God will clear
your blurred vision, you'll see it yet!

Philippians 3:15,16 MSG

More Ideas About . . .
COMMITMENT

There is no more lovely, friendly, and charming
relationship, communion, or company
than a good marriage.

Martin Luther

Success, in a ministry or a marriage, is not the key.
Faithfulness is.

Joni Eareckson Tada

Married life offers no panacea—if it is going to reach
its potential, it will require an all-out investment
by both husband and wife.

James Dobson

As I grew older, I realized that my parents' love for
one another was deeper than just the look in their
eyes each time one of them came into the room.
Their love was based on more than their physical
and emotional attraction. It was based on solid,
uncompromising commitment, first to Jesus Christ,
and second to the institution of marriage.

Gigi Graham Tchividjian

A TIP

It takes time to build a friendship . . .
including the friendship with your spouse.

A PRAYER

We thank You, Lord, for the gift of marriage.
And we thank You for the love, the care,
the devotion, and the genuine friendship that
we share this day and forever.
Amen

COOPERATION

But whosoever will be great among you, let him be your
minister; and whosoever will be chief among you,
let him be your servant: even as the Son of man
came not to be ministered unto, but to minister,
and to give his life a ransom for many.

Matthew 20:26-28 KJV

Have you and your loved one learned the fine art of cooperation? If so, you have learned the wisdom of "give and take," not the foolishness of "me first." Cooperation is the art of compromising on little things while keeping your eye on the big thing: your relationship.

Cooperative relationships grow and flourish over time. But, when couples fail to cooperate, they unintentionally sow seeds of dissatisfaction and disharmony.

If you're like most of us, you're probably a little bit headstrong: you probably want most things done in a fashion resembling the popular song "My Way." But, if you are observant, you will notice that those people who always insist upon "my way or the highway" usually end up with "the highway."

A better strategy for all concerned is to abandon the search for "my way" and search instead for "our way." That tune has a far happier ending.

A TIP

Cooperation pays. When you cooperate with
your friends and family, you'll feel good
about yourself—and your family and friends
will feel good about you, too.

---

*But a Samaritan, as he traveled, came where the man
was; and when he saw him, he took pity on him.
He went to him and bandaged his wounds, pouring on
oil and wine. Then he put the man on his own donkey,
took him to an inn and took care of him.*

Luke 10:33-34 NIV

Promises from God's Word About . . .
SERVING EACH OTHER

So prepare your minds for service and have self-control.

1 Peter 1:13 NCV

Let this mind be in you which was also in Christ Jesus, who . . . made Himself of no reputation, taking the form of a bondservant, and coming in the likeness of men.

Philippians 2:5,7 NKJV

Therefore, since we receive a kingdom which cannot be shaken, let us show gratitude, by which we may offer to God an acceptable service with reverence and awe....

Hebrews 12:28 NASB

Suppose a brother or a sister is without clothes and daily food. If one of you says to him, "Go, I wish you well; keep warm and well fed," but does nothing about his physical needs, what good is it?

James 2:15-16 NIV

More Ideas About . . .
SERVING EACH OTHER

Being committed to one's mate is not a matter of demanding rights, but a matter of releasing rights.

Charles Swindoll

Cooperation is a two-way street, but for too many couples, it's the road less traveled.

Marie T. Freeman

We worship God through service.
The authentic server views each opportunity to lead or serve as an opportunity to worship God.

Bill Hybels

You get the most out of your work when you view yourself as a servant.

Charles Stanley

You can judge how far you have risen in the scale of life by asking one question: How wisely and how deeply do I care? To be Christianized is to be sensitized. Christians are people who care.

E. Stanley Jones

Promises from God's Word About . . .
COOPERATION AND SERVICE

But he who is greatest among you shall be your servant.

Matthew 23:11 NKJV

The righteous give and don't hold back.

Proverbs 21:26 Holman CSB

*When it is in your power, don't withhold good
from the one to whom it is due.*

Proverbs 3:27 Holman CSB

*The generous soul will be made rich,
and he who waters will also be watered himself.*

Proverbs 11:25 NKJV

*If anyone serves Me, let him follow Me;
and where I am, there My servant will be also.
If anyone serves Me, him My Father will honor.*

John 12:26 NKJV

More Ideas About . . .
COOPERATION AND SERVICE

In the very place where God has put us, whatever its
limitations, whatever kind of work it may be,
we may indeed serve the Lord Christ.

Elisabeth Elliot

Christians are like the flowers in a garden: they have
upon them the dew of heaven, which, being shaken
by the wind, they let fall at each other's roots,
whereby they are jointly nourished.

John Bunyan

If the attitude of servanthood is learned, by
attending to God as Lord. Then, serving others
will develop as a very natural way of life.

Eugene Peterson

Do things for others and you'll find your
self-consciousness evaporating like morning dew
on a Missouri cornfield in July.

Dale Carnegie

A TIP

A willingness to serve others is
a sign of greatness in God's eyes.

A PRAYER

Dear Lord, give me a servant's heart.
When Jesus humbled Himself and became a servant,
He also became an example for His followers.
Make me a faithful steward of my gifts,
and let me share with those in need.
Amen

ENCOURAGEMENT

So encourage each other and give each other strength,
just as you are doing now.

1 Thessalonians 5:11 NCV

Marriage is a team sport, and all of us need occasional pats on the back from our teammate. In the Book of Proverbs, we read that, "A word aptly spoken is like apples of gold in settings of silver" (25:11 NIV). This verse reminds us that the words we speak can and should be beautiful offerings to those we love.

All of us have the power to enrich the lives of our loved ones. Sometimes, when we feel uplifted and secure, we find it easy to speak words of encouragement and hope. Other times, when we are discouraged or tired, we can scarcely summon the energy to uplift ourselves, much less anyone else. But, as loving Christians, our obligation is clear: we must always measure our words carefully as we use them to benefit others and to glorify our Father in heaven.

God intends that we speak words of kindness, wisdom, and truth, no matter our circumstances, no matter our emotions. When we do, we share a priceless gift with our loved ones, and we give glory to the One who gave His life for us. As believers, we must do no less.

A TIP

When talking to other people, ask yourself
this question: "How helpful can I be?"

Encourage each other.
Live in harmony and peace.
Then the God of love and peace
will be with you.

2 Corinthians 13:11 NLT

Promises from God's Word About . . .
ENCOURAGEMENT

*Let's see how inventive we can be in encouraging love
and helping out, not avoiding worshipping together as
some do but spurring each other on.*

Hebrews 10:24-25 MSG

*Watch the way you talk. Let nothing foul or dirty come
out of your mouth. Say only what helps,
each word a gift.*

Ephesians 4:29 MSG

*Let the word of Christ dwell in you richly in all wisdom;
teaching and admonishing one another in psalms and
hymns and spiritual songs, singing with grace
in your hearts to the Lord.*

Colossians 3:16 KJV

*But encourage one another day after day, as long as it is
still called "Today," so that none of you will be
hardened by the deceitfulness of sin.*

Hebrews 3:13 NASB

More Ideas About . . .
ENCOURAGEMENT

What are your spouse's dreams? What are you doing
to encourage or discourage those dreams?

Dennis Swanberg

Encouragement is to a friendship what
confetti is to a party.

Nicole Johnson

God of our life, there are days when the burdens
we carry chafe our shoulders and weigh us down;
when the road seems dreary and endless, the skies
gray and threatening; when our lives have no music
in them, and our hearts are lonely, and our souls
have lost their courage. Flood the path with light,
run our eyes to where the skies are full of promise;
tune our hearts to brave music; give us the sense of
comradeship with heroes and saints of every age;
and so quicken our spirits that we may be able to
encourage the souls of all who journey with us on
the road of life, to Your honor and glory.

St. Augustine

Promises from God's Word About . . .
KIND WORDS

*To everything there is a season...a time to keep silence,
and a time to speak.*

Ecclesiastes 3:1, 7 KJV

For out of the overflow of the heart the mouth speaks.

Matthew 12:34 NIV

*But I say unto you, That every idle word that men
shall speak, they shall give account thereof in the day of
judgment. For by thy words thou shalt be justified,
and by thy words thou shalt be condemned.*

Matthew 12:36-37 KJV

*Reckless words pierce like a sword, but the tongue
of the wise brings healing.*

Proverbs 12:18 NIV

*Let the words of my mouth, and the meditations of
my heart, be acceptable in thy sight, O Lord,
my strength and my redeemer.*

Psalm 19:14 KJV

More Ideas About . . .
KIND WORDS

To rejoice at another person's joy is like
being in heaven.

Meister Eckhart

To the loved, a word of affection is a morsel,
but to the love-starved,
a word of affection can be a feast.

Max Lucado

If someone listens or stretches out a hand or
whispers a word of encouragement or attempts to
understand a lonely person, extraordinary things
begin to happen.

Loretta Girzartis

Words. Do you fully understand their power? Can
any of us really grasp the mighty force behind the
things we say? Do we stop and think before we
speak, considering the potency of the words we
utter?

Joni Eareckson Tada

A TIP

Sometimes, even a very few words can make
a very big difference. As Fanny Crosby observed,
"A single word, if spoken in a friendly spirit,
may be sufficient to turn one from dangerous error."

A PRAYER

Lord, make us mindful of our words. This world can
be a difficult place, and many of Your children are
discouraged and afraid. Make each member of our
family a powerful source of encouragement to those
in need, and let our words and deeds be worthy
of Your Son, the One who gives us courage and
strength, this day and for all eternity.
Amen

FORGIVENESS

Be even-tempered, content with second place, quick to forgive an offense. Forgive as quickly and completely as the Master forgave you. And regardless of what else you put on, wear love. It's your basic, all-purpose garment. Never be without it.

Colossians 3:13-14 MSG

If we want to make love last forever, we must learn the art of forgiveness. Why? Because our loved ones are imperfect (as are we). How often must we forgive our spouses? More times than we can count. In other words, we must not just learn how to forgive; we must learn how to keep forgiving (Matthew 18:21-22).

Perhaps granting forgiveness is hard for you. If so, you are not alone. Granting heartfelt forgiveness is often difficult—difficult but not impossible.

When it comes to the hard work of forgiving those who have injured us, God is willing to help, but He expects us to do some of the work—and when we do so, we are blessed.

When we forgive others, we gain the peace that God offers those who obey His Word. But when we harbor bitterness against others, we forfeit that peace—and by doing so, we bring needless harm to ourselves and to our loved ones. So, if there exists even one person, alive or dead, whom you have not forgiven (and that includes yourself or your spouse), follow God's commandment—forgive. Because bitterness, anger, and regret are emotions that have no place in your life or your marriage.

A TIP

When other people have made a mistake . . .
it's a mistake not to forgive them.

*But if you harbor bitter envy and selfish ambition in
your hearts, do not boast about it or deny the truth.
Such "wisdom" does not come down from heaven but
is earthly, unspiritual, of the devil. For where you have
envy and selfish ambition, there you find
disorder and every evil practice.*

James 3:14-16 NIV

Promises from God's Word About . . .
FORGIVENESS

Have mercy on me, O God, according to your unfailing love; according to your great compassion blot out my transgressions. Wash away all my iniquity and cleanse me from my sin.

Psalm 51:1-2 NIV

If you forgive those who sin against you, your heavenly Father will forgive you. But if you refuse to forgive others, your Father will not forgive your sins.

Matthew 6:14-15 NLT

And be ye kind one to another, tenderhearted, forgiving one another, even as God for Christ's sake hath forgiven you.

Ephesians 4:32 KJV

Whenever you stand praying, forgive, if you have anything against anyone, so that your Father in heaven will also forgive you your transgressions.

Mark 11:25 NASB

More Ideas About . . .
FORGIVENESS

Every time we forgive others, deserving it or not,
we have a reminder of God's forgiveness.

Franklin Graham

The well of God's forgiveness never runs dry.

Grady Nutt

Having forgiven, I am liberated.

Father Lawrence Jenco

Give me such love for God and men as will
blot out all hatred and bitterness.

Dietrich Bonhoeffer

Man lives by getting and forgetting.
God lives by giving and forgiving.

Diana Baskin

Promises from God's Word About . . .
BITTERNESS AND REGRET

*All bitterness, anger and wrath, insult and slander must
be removed from you, along with all wickedness.
And be kind and compassionate to one another, forgiving
one another, just as God also forgave you in Christ.*

Ephesians 4:31-32 Holman CSB

*But now you must also put away all the following:
anger, wrath, malice, slander, and filthy language
from your mouth.*

Colossians 3:8 Holman CSB

*Do not repay anyone evil for evil.
Try to do what is honorable in everyone's eyes.*

Romans 12:17 Holman CSB

*The Lord says, "Forget what happened before, and do
not think about the past. Look at the new thing I am
going to do. It is already happening.
Don't you see it? I will make a road in
the desert and rivers in the dry land."*

Isaiah 43:18-19 NCV

More Ideas About . . .
BITTERNESS AND REGRET

Forgiveness does not mean the perpetrator
goes free; it means that the forgiver is free and
that God will justly deal with those
who have caused pain.

Cynthia Heald

When God forgives, He forgets. He buries our sins
in the sea and puts a sign on the shore saying,
"No Fishing Allowed."

Corrie ten Boom

Get rid of the poison of built-up anger and
the acid of long-term resentment

Charles Swindoll

Forgiveness is the precondition of love.

Catherine Marshall

Only the truly forgiven are truly forgiving.

C. S. Lewis

A TIP

Forgive . . . and keep forgiving! Sometimes,
forgiveness is a journey. That means that you may
forgive someone once and then, at a later time,
become angry at the very same person again.
If so, you must forgive that person again
and again . . . until it sticks!

A PRAYER

Dear Lord, sometimes forgiveness is difficult indeed.
Today, Father, I ask You to help me move beyond
feelings of bitterness and anger. Jesus forgave those
who hurt Him; let me walk in His footsteps by
forgiving those who have injured me.
Amen

PATIENCE

Patience of spirit is better than haughtiness of spirit.

Ecclesiastes 7:8 NASB

Marriage is an exercise in patience. From time to time, even the most considerate spouse may do things that worry us, or confuse us, or anger us. Why? Because even the most considerate spouse is still an imperfect human being, capable of missteps, misdeeds, and mistakes. And it is precisely because our loved ones are human that we learn to be patient with their shortcomings (just as they, too, must be patient with ours).

Are you one of those people who demand perfection from everybody, with the possible exception of yourself? If so, it's time to reassess your expectations. God doesn't expect perfection, and neither should you.

Proverbs 19:11 makes it clear: "People with good sense restrain their anger; they earn esteem by overlooking wrongs" (NLT). So the next time you find yourself drumming your fingers while waiting for your loved one to do the right thing, take a deep breath and ask God for patience. After all, the world unfolds according to God's timetable, not yours. And your loved ones live—and grow—according to their own timetables, too. Sometimes, you must wait patiently, and that's as it should be. After all, think how patient God has been with you.

A TIP

Be patient . . . very patient. Want them to be
patient with you? Then you must do the same for
them. Never expect other people to be more patient
with you than you are with them.

It is wise to wait because God gives
clear direction only when we are
willing to wait.

Charles Stanley

Promises from God's Word About . . .
PATIENCE

Patience is better than strength.

Proverbs 16:32 ICB

Patience and encouragement come from God.
And I pray that God will help you all agree with
each other the way Christ Jesus wants.

Romans 15:5 NCV

But if we look forward to something we don't have yet,
we must wait patiently and confidently.

Romans 8:25 NLT

The Lord is wonderfully good to those who wait for him
and seek him. So it is good to wait quietly for
salvation from the Lord.

Lamentations 3:25-26 NLT

Wait on the Lord; Be of good courage, and He shall
strengthen your heart; Wait, I say, on the Lord!

Psalm 27:14 NKJV

More Ideas About . . .
PATIENCE

God never hurries. There are no deadlines against
which He must work. To know this is to quiet our
spirits and relax our nerves.

A. W. Tozer

Those who have had to wait and work for happiness
seem to enjoy it more, because they
never take it for granted.

Barbara Johnson

As we wait on God, He helps us use the winds of
adversity to soar above our problems.
As the Bible says, "Those who wait on the Lord…
shall mount up with wings like eagles."

Billy Graham

By his wisdom, he orders his delays so that they
prove to be far better than our hurries.

C. H. Spurgeon

Promises from God's Word About . . .
BEING PATIENT AND UNDERSTANDING

Here is a simple, rule-of-thumb for behavior:
Ask yourself what you want people to do for you,
then grab the initiative and do it for them. Add up
God's Law and Prophets and this is what you get.

Matthew 7:12 MSG

So, as those who have been chosen of God,
holy and beloved, put on a heart of compassion,
kindness, humility, gentleness and patience.

Colossians 3:12 NASB

Be hospitable to one another without complaining.

1 Peter 4:9 Holman CSB

And be ye kind one to another, tenderhearted,
forgiving one another, even as God for Christ's
sake hath forgiven you.

Ephesians 4:32 KJV

More Ideas About . . .
BEING PATIENT AND UNDERSTANDING

God is in no hurry. Compared to the works of
mankind, He is extremely deliberate.
God is not a slave to the human clock.

Charles Swindoll

He makes us wait. He keeps us in the dark on
purpose. He makes us walk when we want to run,
sit still when we want to walk, for he has things to
do in our souls that we are not interested in.

Elisabeth Elliot

In all negotiations of difficulties, a man may not
look to sow and reap at once. He must prepare his
business and so ripen it by degrees.

Francis Bacon

When we read of the great Biblical leaders, we see
that it was not uncommon for God to ask them to
wait, not just a day or two, but for years,
until God was ready for them to act.

Gloria Gaither

A TIP

God has been patient with you . . .
now it's your turn to be patient with others.

A PRAYER

Lord, I am tempted to rush through my day scarcely
giving a thought to the blessings You have given me.
There seem to be so many things to accomplish and
so little time, Lord, and I am often impatient.
Slow me down, Father, and keep me mindful that
the world is Your creation and that it unfolds
according to Your plans. Let me trust Your plans,
Lord, with patience and thanksgiving,
today and always.
Amen

AVOID PERFECTIONISM

*Those who wait for perfect weather will never plant
seeds; those who look at every cloud will never harvest
crops. Plant early in the morning, and work until
evening, because you don't know if this or that will
succeed. They might both do well.*

Ecclesiastes 11:4,6 NCV

Expectations, expectations, expectations! As a dues-paying citizen of the 21st century, you know that demands can be high, and expectations even higher. The media delivers an endless stream of messages that tell you how to look, how to behave, how to eat, and how to dress. The media's expectations are impossible to meet—God's are not. God doesn't expect perfection . . . and neither should you.

The difference between perfectionism and realistic expectations is the difference between a life of frustration and a life of contentment. Only one earthly being ever lived life to perfection, and He was the Son of God. The rest of us have fallen short of God's standard and need to be accepting of our own limitations as well as the limitations of others.

If you find you or your spouse are bound up by the chains of perfectionism, it's time to ask yourself who you're trying to impress, and why. If you're trying to impress your friends, or if you're trying to imitate the appearance of some rail-thin Hollywood celebrity, it's time to reconsider your priorities. Your first responsibility is to the heavenly Father who created you and to the Son who saved you. Then, you bear a powerful responsibility to your spouse and your family. But, when it comes to meeting society's unrealistic expectations, forget it!

Remember that when you accepted Christ as your Savior, God accepted you for all eternity. Now, it's your turn to accept yourself and your loved ones. When you do, you'll feel a tremendous weight being lifted from your shoulders. After all, pleasing God is simply a matter of obeying His commandments and accepting His Son. But as for pleasing everybody else? That's impossible!

A TIP

Accept your own imperfections:
If you're caught up in the modern-day push
toward perfection, grow up . . .
and then lighten up on yourself.

Promises from God's Word About . . .
PERFECTIONISM

*Your beliefs about these things should be kept secret
between you and God. People are happy if they can do
what they think is right without feeling guilty.*

Romans 14:22 NCV

*The fear of human opinion disables;
trusting in God protects you from that.*

Proverbs 29:25 MSG

*In thee, O Lord, do I put my trust;
let me never be put into confusion.*

Psalm 71:1 KJV

*Teach me Your way, O Lord;
I will walk in Your truth.*

Psalm 86:11 NASB

More Ideas About . . .
PERFECTIONISM

Walk in the good, believe in God, don't try to
acquire perfection by force, but do everything
quietly and then you will be truly humble.
Then, God will give you everything.

Paul of the Cross

God is not hard to please. He does not expect us
to be absolutely perfect. He just expects us to keep
moving toward Him and believing in Him,
letting Him work with us to bring us into
conformity to His will and ways.

Joyce Meyer

A good garden may have some weeds.

Thomas Fuller

As perfectionists we find it difficult, if not
impossible, to believe that God could completely
accept, love, and long to be with us
in this unfinished state.

Susan Lenzkes

Promises from God's Word About . . .
SUCCESS

Success, success to you, and success to those who help you, for your God will help you....

1 Chronicles 12:18 NIV

But as for you, be strong and do not give up, for your work will be rewarded.

2 Chronicles 15:7 NIV

Let us not become weary in doing good, for at the proper time we will reap a harvest if we do not give up.

Galatians 6:9 NIV

You need to persevere so that when you have done the will of God, you will receive what he has promised.

Hebrews 10:36 NIV

The one who understands a matter finds success, and the one who trusts in the Lord will be happy.

Proverbs 16:20 Holman CSB

More Ideas About . . .
SUCCESS

We shall never come to the perfect man
til we come to the perfect world.

Matthew Henry

Nothing would be done at all, if a man waited
until he could do it so well that no one
could find fault with it.

John Henry Cardinal Newman

The happiest people in the world are not those who
have no problems, but the people who have learned
to live with those things that are less than perfect.

James Dobson

God is so inconceivably good. He's not looking
for perfection. He already saw it in Christ.
He's looking for affection.

Beth Moore

Perfection consists simply in . . .
being just what God wants us to be.

Therese of Lisieux

A TIP

Don't be too hard on yourself.
You don't have to be perfect to be wonderful.

A PRAYER

Dear Lord, I'm certainly not perfect,
but You love me anyway.
Thank You for Your love, and for Your Son.
Amen

KEEP POSSESSIONS IN PERSPECTIVE

Do not love the world or the things in the world.
If anyone loves the world,
the love of the Father is not in him.

1 John 2:15 NKJV

Earthly riches are temporary. Spiritual riches, on the other hand, are everlasting. Yet all too often, we focus our thoughts and energies on the accumulation of earthly treasures, leaving precious little time for anything else.

Far too many marriages are weighted down by endless concerns about money and possessions. Too many couples mistakenly focus their thoughts and efforts on newer cars, better clothes, and bigger houses. The results of these misplaced priorities are always unfortunate, and sometimes tragic.

Certainly we all need the basic necessities of life, but once we meet those needs for our families and ourselves, the piling up of possessions creates more problems than it solves. Our real riches are not of this world: we are never really rich until we are rich in spirit.

Do you find yourself wrapped up in the concerns of the material world? If so, it's time for you and your spouse to sit down and have a heart-to-heart talk about "stuff." When you do, you should reorder your priorities by turning away from materialism and back to God. Then, you can begin storing up riches that will endure throughout eternity: the spiritual kind.

A TIP

Materialism Made Simple: The world wants you to believe that "money and stuff" can buy happiness. Don't believe it! Genuine happiness comes not from money, but from the things that money can't buy—starting, of course, with your relationship to God and His only begotten Son.

He who trusts in his riches will fall, but the righteous will flourish . . . .

Proverbs 11:28 NKJV

Promises from God's Word About . . .
MATERIALISM

*And He told them, "Watch out and be on guard
against all greed, because one's life is not in
the abundance of his possessions.*

Luke 12:15 Holman CSB

*No one can serve two masters. The person will hate
one master and love the other, or will follow one master
and refuse to follow the other. You cannot serve
both God and worldly riches.*

Matthew 6:24 NCV

*For the mind-set of the flesh is death,
but the mind-set of the Spirit is life and peace.*

Romans 8:6 Holman CSB

*Since we entered the world penniless and will leave it
penniless, if we have bread on the table
and shoes on our feet, that's enough.*

1 Timothy 6:7-8 MSG

More Ideas About . . .
MATERIALISM

It's sobering to contemplate how much time, effort,
sacrifice, compromise, and attention we give to
acquiring and increasing our supply of something
that is totally insignificant in eternity.

Anne Graham Lotz

If you want to be truly happy, you won't find it
on an endless quest for more stuff. You'll find it in
receiving God's generosity and in the passing
that generosity along.

Bill Hybels

There is absolutely no evidence that complexity
and materialism lead to happiness. On the contrary,
there is plenty of evidence that simplicity and
spirituality lead to joy, a blessedness that is
better than happiness.

Dennis Swanberg

Greed is enslaving. The more you have, the more
you want—until eventually avarice consumes you.

Kay Arthur

Promises from God's Word About . . .
MANAGING MONEY WISELY

*For the love of money is a root of all sorts of evil,
and some by longing for it have wandered away from
the faith and pierced themselves with many griefs.*

1 Timothy 6:10 NASB

*Do not love the world or the things in the world.
If anyone loves the world,
the love of the Father is not in him.*

1 John 2:15 NKJV

*For what will it profit a man if he gains
the whole world, and loses his own soul?
Or what will a man give in exchange for his soul?*

Mark 8:36-37 NKJV

*For where your treasure is,
there your heart will be also.*

Luke 12:34 NKJV

More Ideas About . . .
MANAGING MONEY WISELY

Outside appearances, things like the clothes you
wear or the car you drive, are important to other
people but totally unimportant to God. Trust God.

Marie T. Freeman

We are made spiritually lethargic by
a steady diet of materialism.

Mary Morrison Suggs

A society that pursues pleasure runs the risk of
raising expectations ever higher, so that true
contentment always lies tantalizingly out of reach.

Philip Yancey and Paul Brand

The socially prescribed affluent, middle-class
lifestyle has become so normative in our churches
that we discern little conflict between it
and the Christian lifestyle prescribed
in the New Testament.

Tony Compolo

A TIP

Too Much Stuff: Too much stuff doesn't ensure happiness. In fact, having too much stuff can actually prevent happiness.

A PRAYER

Dear Lord, help me remember that the things in this world that are really valuable are my life, my family, and my relationship with You.
Amen

PRAY TOGETHER

The intense prayer of the righteous is very powerful.

James 5:16 Holman CSB

I s prayer an integral part of your married life or is it a hit-or-miss habit? Do you and your spouse "pray without ceasing," or is prayer usually an afterthought? Do you regularly pray together, or do you only bow your heads in unison during Sunday morning services? The answer to these questions determine the quality of your prayer life and, to a surprising extent, the spiritual strength of your marriage.

Andrew Murray observed, "Some people pray just to pray, and some people pray to know God." Your task, along with your spouse, is to pray together, not out of habit or obligation, but out of a sincere desire to know your Heavenly Father.

Through constant prayers, you and your spouse should petition God, you should praise God, and you should seek God's guidance for your marriage and your life.

Prayer changes things, prayer changes people, and prayer changes marriages. So don't limit your prayers to meals or to bedtime. Pray constantly about things great and small. God is listening, and He wants to hear from you—and your spouse—right now.

A TIP

Prayer strengthens your relationship with God . . .
So Pray. Beth Moore writes,
"Prayer keeps us in constant communion with God,
which is the goal of our entire believing lives."
It's up to you to live—and pray—accordingly.

---

*I want men everywhere to lift up holy hands
in prayer, without anger or disputing.*

1 Timothy 2:8 NIV

Promises from God's Word About . . .
THE POWER OF PRAYER

*And everything—whatever you ask in prayer,
believing—you will receive.*

Matthew 21:22 Holman CSB

*Therefore I want the men in every place to pray,
lifting up holy hands without anger or argument.*

1 Timothy 2:8 Holman CSB

The intense prayer of the righteous is very powerful.

James 5:16 Holman CSB

Yet He often withdrew to deserted places and prayed.

Luke 5:16 Holman CSB

More Ideas About . . .
THE POWER OF PRAYER

God is always listening.

Stormie Omartian

Because God is eternal,
pray boldly and live confidently.

Stanley Grenz

Through prayer, God quickens our spirits by
the power of His Holy Spirit.

Shirley Dobson

Prayer is the most important tool for your mission
to the world. People may refuse our love
or reject our message, but they are
defenseless against our prayers.

Rick Warren

Prayer catapults us onto the frontier of spiritual life.

Richard Foster

Promises from God's Word About . . .
GOD ANSWERS PRAYERS

*"Relax, Daniel,' he continued, 'don't be afraid. From
the moment you decided to humble yourself to receive
understanding, your prayer was heard,
and I set out to come to you.'"*

Daniel 10:12 MSG

*If you don't know what you're doing, pray to
the Father. He loves to help. You'll get his help,
and won't be condescended to when you ask for it.
Ask boldly, believingly, without a second thought.
People who "worry their prayers" are like wind-whipped
waves. Don't think you're going to get anything
from the Master that way, adrift at sea,
keeping all your options open.*

James 1:5-8 MSG

*Rejoice always, pray without ceasing,
in everything give thanks;
for this is the will of God in Christ Jesus for you.*

1 Thessalonians 5:16-18 NKJV

More Ideas About . . .
GOD ANSWERS PRAYERS

What God gives in answer to our prayers will always
be the thing we most urgently need, and it will
always be sufficient.

Elisabeth Elliot

The Lord's answers to prayer are infinitely perfect,
and they will show that often when we were
asking for a stone that looked like bread,
He was giving us bread that to
our shortsightedness looked like stone.

J. Southley

Sometimes God is so touched by what he sees
that he gives us what we need and
not simply that for which we ask.

Max Lucado

Be sure to remember that nothing in your daily life
is so insignificant and so inconsequential that
God will not help you by answering your prayer.

Ole Hallesby

A TIP

Sometimes, the answer is "No."
God doesn't grant all of our requests, nor should He.
We must understand that our prayers are answered
by a sovereign, all-knowing God, and that we must
trust His answers, whether the answer is
"Yes," "No," or "Not Yet."

A PRAYER

Dear Lord, make me a person whose constant
prayers are pleasing to You. Let me come to You
often with concerns both great and small. I trust in
the power of prayer, Father, because prayer changes
things and it changes me. In the quiet moments of
the day, I will open my heart to You. I know that
You are with me always and that You always hear
my prayers. So I will pray and be thankful.
Amen

WATCH YOUR WORDS

Pleasant words are a honeycomb:
sweet to the taste and health to the body.

Proverbs 16:24 Holman CSB

All too often, we underestimate the importance of the words we speak. Whether we realize it or not, our words carry great weight and great power, especially when we are addressing our loved ones.

The Bible reminds us that "Reckless words pierce like a sword, but the tongue of the wise brings healing" (Proverbs 12:18 NIV). And Christ taught that "Out of the abundance of the heart the mouth speaks" (Matthew 12:34 NKJV).

Does the abundance of your heart produce a continuing flow of encouraging words for your loved ones? And, are you willing to hold your tongue when you feel the urge to begin an angry outburst? Hopefully so. After all, sometimes the most important words are the ones you don't speak.

If you want to build a better marriage—and if you want to keep building it day by day—think first and talk next. Avoid angry outbursts. Refrain from constant criticism. Terminate tantrums. Negate negativism. Cease cynicism. Instead, use Christ as your guide, and speak words of encouragement, hope, praise, and, above all, love—and speak them often.

A TIP

Words, words, words . . . are important, important, important! So make sure that you think first and speak next. Otherwise, you may give the greatest speech you wish you'd never made!

Watch the way you talk. Let nothing foul or dirty come out of your mouth. Say only what helps, each word a gift.

Ephesians 4:29 MSG

Promises from God's Word About . . .
THE POWER OF WORDS

*So then, rid yourselves of all evil, all lying, hypocrisy,
jealousy, and evil speech. As newborn babies want milk,
you should want the pure and simple teaching.
By it you can grow up and be saved.*

1 Peter 2:1–2 NCV

*Be gracious in your speech. The goal is to bring out
the best in others in a conversation,
not put them down, not cut them out.*

Colossians 4:6 MSG

*To everything there is a season…a time to keep silence,
and a time to speak.*

Ecclesiastes 3:1, 7 KJV

*If anyone considers himself religious and yet does not
keep a tight rein on his tongue, he deceives himself
and his religion is worthless.*

James 1:26 NIV

More Ideas About . . .
THE POWER OF WORDS

Like dynamite, God's power is only latent power
until it is released. You can release God's dynamite
power into people's lives and the world through
faith, your words, and prayer.

Bill Dright

The things that we feel most deeply we ought to
learn to be silent about, at least until we have talked
them over thoroughly with God.

Elisabeth Elliot

Every word we speak, every action we take, has
an effect on the totality of humanity. No one can
escape that privilege—or that responsibility.

Laurie Beth Jones

We will always experience regret when we live for
the moment and do not weigh our words and deeds
before we give them life.

Lisa Bevere

More Ideas About . . .
COURTESY

*Therefore, my brothers, when you come together to eat,
wait for one another.*

1 Corinthians 11:33 Holman CSB

Be hospitable to one another without grumbling.

1 Peter 4:9 NKJV

*Dear friend, when you extend hospitality to Christian
brothers and sisters, even when they are strangers,
you make the faith visible.*

3 John 1:5 MSG

*Out of respect for Christ, be courteously
reverent to one another.*

Ephesians 5:21 MSG

*Are there those among you who are truly wise and
understanding? Then they should show it by living right
and doing good things with a gentleness
that comes from wisdom.*

James 3:13 NCV

Promises from God's Word About . . .
COURTESY

The great test of a man's character is his tongue.

Oswald Chambers

Perhaps we have been guilty of speaking against someone and have not realized how it may have hurt them. Then when someone speaks against us, we suddenly realize how deeply such words hurt, and we become sensitive to what we have done.

Theodore Epp

I still believe we ought to talk about Jesus. The old country doctor of my boyhood days always began his examination by saying, "Let me see your tongue." That's a good way to check a Christian: the tongue test. Let's hear what he is talking about.

Vance Havner

Change the heart, and you change the speech.

Warren Wiersbe

A TIP

When in doubt, use the Golden Rule to help you decide what to say. If you wouldn't like for somebody to say it about you, don't say it about them!

A PRAYER

Dear Lord, You hear every word that I say.
Let my speech bring honor to You and to Your Son.
Today and every day, let me speak words that are honest, kind, and worthy of You.
Amen

WORSHIP TOGETHER

Worship the Lord your God and . . . serve Him only.

Matthew 4:10 Holman CSB

The old saying is familiar and true: "The family that prays together stays together." And, our world would be a far better place if more husbands and wives spent more time praying together . . . lots more time.

We should never deceive ourselves: every marriage is based upon some form of worship. The question is not whether we worship, but what we worship. Some families choose to worship God. The result is a plentiful harvest of joy, peace, and abundance. Other families distance themselves from God by foolishly worshiping things of this earth such as fame, fortune, or personal gratification. To do so is a terrible mistake with eternal consequences.

Whenever we place our love for material possessions above our love for God—or when we yield to the countless temptations of this world—we find ourselves engaged in a struggle between good and evil, a clash between God and Satan. Our responses to these struggles have implications that echo throughout our families and throughout our communities. How can we ensure that we cast our lot with God? We do so, in part, by committing ourselves to the discipline of regular worship with our families.

Every day provides opportunities to put God where He belongs: at the center of our lives and our marriages. When we do so, we worship not just with our words, but also with deeds, and that's as it should be. For believers, God comes first. Always first.

A TIP

Worship reminds you of the awesome power of God.
So worship Him daily, and allow Him to
work through you every day of the week
(not just on Sunday).

Promises from God's Word About . . .
WORSHIP

A time is coming and has now come when the true
worshipers will worship the Father in spirit and truth,
for they are the kind of worshipers the Father seeks.
God is spirit, and his worshipers must worship
in spirit and in truth.

John 4:23-24 NIV

If any man thirst, let him come unto me, and drink.

John 7:37 KJV

For it is written, "You shall worship the Lord your God,
and Him only you shall serve."

Matthew 4:10 NKJV

But seek first his kingdom and his righteousness,
and all these things will be given to you as well.

Matthew 6:33 NIV

More Ideas About . . .
WORSHIP

It's our privilege to not only raise our hands in
worship but also to combine the visible with the
invisible in a rising stream of praise and
adoration sent directly to our Father.

Shirley Dobson

O worship the King, all glorious above,
And gratefully sing His wonderful love.

Robert Grant

When God is at the center of your life, you worship.
When he's not, you worry.

Rick Warren

Worship is our response to the overtures of love
from the heart of the Father.

Richard Foster

Worship is about rekindling an ashen heart
into a blazing fire.

Liz Curtis Higgs

Promises from God's Word About . . .
PRAISE

Is anyone happy? Let him sing songs of praise.

James 5:13 NIV

*Through Him then, let us continually offer up a sacrifice
of praise to God, that is, the fruit of lips
that give thanks to His name.*

Hebrews 13:15 NASB

*The Lord is my strength and song,
and He has become my salvation;
He is my God, and I will praise Him.*

Exodus 15:2 NIV

*And suddenly there was with the angel a multitude of
the heavenly host praising God and saying:
"Glory to God in the highest,
And on earth peace, goodwill toward men!"*

Luke 2:13-14 NKJV

More Ideas About . . .
PRAISE

In the sanctuary, we discover beauty:
the beauty of His presence.

Kay Arthur

Worship is a lifestyle.

Joey Johnson

Worship is not taught from the pulpit.
It must be learned in the heart.

Jim Elliot

God asks that we worship Him with our
concentrated minds as well as with our wills and
emotions. A divided and scattered mind
is not effective.

Catherine Marshall

A TIP

The best way to worship God . . .
is to worship Him sincerely and often.

A PRAYER

When I worship You, Lord, You direct my path and
You cleanse my heart. Let today and every day be a
time of worship and praise. Let me worship You in
everything that I think and do. Thank You, Lord,
for the priceless gift of Your Son Jesus.
Let me be worthy of that gift, and let me give
You the praise and the glory forever.
Amen

SHARE YOUR DREAMS

*Live full lives, full in the fullness of God. God can do
anything, you know—far more than you could ever
imagine or guess or request in your wildest dreams!
He does it not by pushing us around but by working
within us, his Spirit deeply and gently within us.*

Ephesians 3:19-20 MSG

Are you willing to entertain the possibility that God has big plans for you and for your marriage? Hopefully so. Yet sometimes, especially if you've recently experienced a life-altering disappointment, you may find it difficult to envision a brighter future for yourself or for your family. If so, it's time to reconsider your own capabilities . . . and God's.

Concentration camp survivor Corrie ten Boom observed, "Every experience God gives us, every person he brings into our lives, is the perfect preparation for the future that only he can see." These words apply to you and yours.

Are you excited about the opportunities of today and thrilled by the possibilities of tomorrow? Do you confidently expect God to lead you to a place of abundance, peace, and joy? And, when your days on earth are over, do you expect to receive the priceless gift of eternal life? If you trust God's promises, and if you have welcomed God's Son into your heart, then you believe that your future is intensely and eternally bright.

Your heavenly Father created you and your loved ones with unique gifts and untapped talents; your job is to tap them. When you do, you'll begin to feel an increasing sense of confidence in yourself and in your future.

It takes courage to dream big dreams and even more courage to share them. You will discover that kind of courage when you do three things: accept the past, trust God to handle the future, and make the most of the time He has given you today. Nothing is too difficult for God, and no dreams are too big for Him—not even yours. So start living—and dreaming—accordingly.

Dreams are wonderful things to share. Have you shared yours lately? Hopefully so. But if you've been hesitant to give voice to your hopes and dreams, remember this: dreaming works best when it's a team sport.

A TIP

Trust God and believe in yourself:
You can do BIG things if you believe
you can do BIG things.

Promises from God's Word About . . .
DREAMS

I came so they can have real and eternal life,
more and better life than they ever dreamed of.

John 10:10 MSG

It is pleasant to see dreams come true,
but fools will not turn from evil to attain them.

Proverbs 13:19 NLT

Where there is no vision, the people perish....

Proverbs 29:18 KJV

Be of good courage, and he shall strengthen your heart,
all ye that hope in the Lord.

Psalm 31:24 KJV

More Ideas About . . .
DREAMS

The future lies all before us. Shall it only be a slight
advance upon what we usually do? Ought it not to
be a bound, a leap forward to altitudes of endeavor
and success undreamed of before?

Annie Armstrong

Set goals so big that unless God helps you,
you will be a miserable failure.

Bill Bright

Always stay connected to people and seek out things
that bring you joy. Dream with abandon.
Pray confidently.

Barbara Johnson

To make your dream come true,
you have to stay awake.

Dennis Swanberg

You cannot out-dream God.

John Eldredge

Promises from God's Word About . . .
HOPE

But if we hope for what we do not see,
we eagerly wait for it with patience.

Romans 8:25 Holman CSB

Now may the God of hope fill you with all joy
and peace in believing, so that you may overflow with
hope by the power of the Holy Spirit.

Romans 15:13 Holman CSB

Rejoice in hope; be patient in affliction;
be persistent in prayer.

Romans 12:12 Holman CSB

Lord, I turn my hope to You. My God, I trust in You.
Do not let me be disgraced;
do not let my enemies gloat over me.

Psalms 25:1-2 Holman CSB

Let us hold on to the confession of our hope without
wavering, for He who promised is faithful.

Hebrews 10:23 Holman CSB

More Ideas About . . .
HOPE

We must be willing to give up every dream
but God's dream.

Larry Crabb

Sometimes our dreams were so big
that it took two people to dream them.

Marie T. Freeman

I discovered that sorrow was not to be feared but
rather endured with hope and expectancy that
God would use it to visit and bless my life.

Jill Briscoe

Hope is the power of being cheerful in
circumstances which we know to be desperate.

G. K. Chesterton

Hope is the desire and the ability to move forward.

Emilie Barnes

A TIP

Never be afraid to hope—or to ask—for a miracle.

A PRAYER

Dear Lord, give me the courage to dream
and the faithfulness to trust in Your perfect plan.
When I am worried or weary, give me strength for
today and hope for tomorrow. Keep me mindful of
Your healing power, Your infinite love,
and Your eternal salvation.
Amen

CELEBRATION

Celebrate God all day, every day.
I mean, revel in him!

Philippians 4:4 MSG

Are you living the triumphant life that God has promised? Or are you, instead, a spiritual shrinking violet? As you ponder that question, consider this: God does not intend that you live a life that is commonplace or mediocre. And He doesn't want you hide your light "under a basket." Instead, He wants you to "Let your light so shine before men, that they may see your good works and glorify your Father in heaven" (Matthew 5:16 NKJV). In short, God wants you to live a triumphant life so that others might know precisely what it means to be a believer.

If you're a believer whose passion for Christ is evident for all to see, congratulations. But if you're plagued by the temptations and distractions of these troubled times—or if you've allowed the inevitable frustrations of everyday life to obscure the joy that is rightfully yours—it's time to recharge your spiritual batteries.

C. H. Spurgeon, the renowned 19th century English clergymen, advised, "The Lord is glad to open the gate to every knocking soul. It opens very freely; its hinges are not rusted; no bolts secure it.

Have faith and enter at this moment through holy courage. If you knock with a heavy heart, you shall yet sing with joy of spirit. Never be discouraged!"

Are you doing your best to live each day as a joyful servant of Christ? And, are you inviting your spouse to join in the celebration? Hopefully so. After all, few things in life are more glorious than the joining together of two joyful believers. So now, with no further ado, thank God for your marriage, and let the celebration begin!

A TIP

If you don't feel like celebrating, start counting your blessings. Before long, you'll realize that you have plenty of reasons to celebrate.

Promises from God's Word About . . .
CELEBRATION

*David and the whole house of Israel were celebrating
with all their might before the Lord, with songs and with
harps, lyres, tambourines, sistrums and cymbals.*

2 Samuel 6:5 NIV

*At the dedication of the wall of Jerusalem, the Levites
were sought out from where they lived and were brought
to Jerusalem to celebrate joyfully the dedication
with songs of thanksgiving and with the music of
cymbals, harps and lyres.*

Nehemiah 12:27 NIV

*Delight thyself also in the Lord;
and he shall give thee the desires of thine heart.*

Psalm 37:4 KJV

*Shout for joy to the Lord, all the earth.
Worship the Lord with gladness;
come before him with joyful songs.*

Psalm 100:1-2 NIV

More Ideas About . . .
CELEBRATION

I know nothing, except what everyone knows—
if there when God dances, I should dance.

W. H. Auden

All our life is a celebration for us; we are convinced,
in fact, that God is always everywhere. We sing
while we work…we pray while we carry out
all life's other occupations.

St. Clement of Alexandria

Some of us seem so anxious about avoiding hell
that we forget to celebrate our journey
toward heaven.

Philip Yancey

Celebration is possible only through the deep
realization that life and death are never found
completely separate. Celebration can really come
about only where fear and love, joy and sorrow, tear
and smiles can exist together.

Henri Nouwen

Promises from God's Word About . . .
JOY

Let the hearts of those who seek the Lord rejoice.
Look to the Lord and his strength; seek his face always.

1 Chronicles 16:10-11 NIV

Rejoice evermore. Pray without ceasing.
In every thing give thanks: for this is the will of
God in Christ Jesus concerning you.

1 Thessalonians 5:16-18 KJV

These things I have spoken to you,
that My joy may remain in you,
and that your joy may be full.

John 15:11 NKJV

Always be full of joy in the Lord.
I say it again—rejoice!

Philippians 4:4 NLT

More Ideas About . . .
JOY

If you can forgive the person you were,
accept the person you are, and believe in
the person you will become, you are headed for joy.
So celebrate your life.

Barbara Johnson

Every morning is a fresh opportunity to find
God's extraordinary joy in the most ordinary places.

Janet. L. Weaver

Joy comes from knowing God loves me and
knows who I am and where I'm going . . .
that my future is secure as I rest in Him.

James Dobson

To choose joy means the determination to
let whatever takes place bring us one step
closer to the God of life.

Henri Nouwen

A TIP

Today is a cause for celebration: Psalm 118: 24
has clear instructions for the coming day:
"This is the day which the Lord has made;
let us rejoice and be glad in it."
Plan your day—and your life—accordingly.

A PRAYER

Lord, Your desire is that I be complete in Your joy.
Joy begets celebration. Today, I celebrate the life
and the work You have given me, and I celebrate
the lives of my friends and family. Thank You,
Father, for Your love, for Your blessings,
and for Your joy. Let me treasure Your gifts
and share them this day and forever.
Amen

PERSEVERANCE

*For you need endurance, so that after you have done
God's will, you may receive what was promised.*

Hebrews 10:36 Holman CSB

Marriage is a marathon, not a sprint—and couples who expect otherwise will be sadly disappointed. That's why husbands and wives need large quantities of patience, forgiveness, hope, and perseverance.

Every marriage and every life has its share of roadblocks and stumbling blocks; these situations require courage and determination. As an example of perfect courage and steadfast determination, we need look no further than our Savior, Jesus Christ.

Jesus finished what He began. Despite the torture He endured, despite the shame of the cross, Jesus was steadfast in His faithfulness to God. We, too, must remain faithful—faithful to God, faithful to our principles, and faithful to our loved ones—especially during times of transition or hardship.

The next time you are tempted to give up on yourself, your duties, or your relationships, ask yourself this question: "What would Jesus have me do?" When you find the answer to that question, you'll know precisely what to do.

A TIP

If things don't work out at first, don't quit.
If you never try, you'll never know
how good you can be.

Let us not become weary in doing good,
for at the proper time we will reap
a harvest if we do not give up.

Galatians 6:9 NIV

Promises from God's Word About . . .
PERSEVERANCE

Thanks be to God! He gives us the victory through our Lord Jesus Christ. Therefore, my dear brothers, stand firm. Let nothing move you. Always give yourselves fully to the work of the Lord, because you know that your labor in the Lord is not in vain.

1 Corinthians 15:57-58 NIV

I do not consider myself yet to have taken hold of it. But one thing I do: Forgetting what is behind and straining toward what is ahead, I press on toward the goal to win the prize for which God has called me heavenward in Christ Jesus.

Philippians 3:13-14 NIV

You need to persevere so that when you have done the will of God, you will receive what he has promised.

Hebrews 10:36 NIV

I have fought a good fight, I have finished my course, I have kept the faith.

2 Timothy 4:7 KJV

More Ideas About . . .
PERSEVERANCE

Failure is one of life's most powerful teachers. How we handle our failures determines whether we're going to simply "get by" in life or "press on."

Beth Moore

By perseverance the snail reached the ark.

C. H. Spurgeon

Battles are won in the trenches, in the grit and grime of courageous determination; they are won day by day in the arena of life.

Charles Swindoll

Only the man who follows the command of Jesus single-mindedly and unresistingly lets his yoke rest upon him, finds his burden easy, and under its gentle pressure receives the power to persevere in the right way.

Dietrich Bonhoeffer

Promises from God's Word About . . .
PERSEVERANCE

*Do you not know that the runners in a stadium all race,
but only one receives the prize? Run in such a way that
you may win. Now everyone who competes exercises
self-control in everything. However, they do it to receive
a perishable crown, but we an imperishable one.*

1 Corinthians 9:24-25 Holman CSB

*But as for you, be strong; don't be discouraged,
for your work has a reward.*

2 Chronicles 15:7 Holman CSB

*So we must not get tired of doing good,
for we will reap at the proper time if we don't give up.*

Galatians 6:9 Holman CSB

*Let us lay aside every weight and the sin that so easily
ensnares us, and run with endurance the race
that lies before us, keeping our eyes on Jesus,
the source and perfecter of our faith.*

Hebrews 12:1-2 Holman CSB

More Ideas About . . .
PERSEVERANCE

All rising to a great place is by a winding stair.

Francis Bacon

Perseverance is more than endurance. It is endurance combined with absolute assurance and certainty that what we are looking for is going to happen.

Oswald Chambers

Keep adding, keep walking, keep advancing; do not stop, do not turn back, do not turn from the straight road.

St. Augustine

You cannot persevere unless there is a trial in your life. There can be no victories without battles; there can be no peaks without valleys. If you want the blessing, you must be prepared to carry the burden and fight the battle. God has to balance privileges with responsibilities, blessings with burdens, or else you and I will become spoiled, pampered children.

Warren Wiersbe

A TIP

Are you being tested? Call upon God. The next time you find your courage tested to the limit, remember that God is as near as your next breath, and remember that He offers strength and comfort to His children. He is your shield, your protector, and your deliverer. Call upon Him in your hour of need and then be comforted. Whatever your challenge, whatever your trouble, God can give you the strength to persevere, and that's exactly what you should ask Him to do.

A PRAYER

Lord, when life is difficult, I am tempted to abandon hope in the future. But You are my God, and I can draw strength from You. When I am exhausted, You energize me. When I am afraid, You give me courage. You are with me, Father, in good times and in bad times. I will persevere in the work that You have placed before me, and I will trust in You forever.
Amen

FRIENDSHIP

*Greater love has no one than this,
that he lay down his life for his friends.*

John 15:13 NIV

D o you want your love to last forever? If so, here's a time-tested prescription for a blissfully happy marriage: make certain that your spouse is your best friend.

Genuine friendship between a husband and wife should be treasured and nurtured. As Christians, we are commanded to love one another. The familiar words of 1 Corinthians 13:2 remind us that love and charity are among God's greatest gifts: "And though I have the gift of prophecy, and understand all mysteries, and all knowledge; and though I have all faith, so that I could remove mountains, and have not charity, I am nothing" (KJV).

Is your spouse your best friend? If so, you are immensely blessed by God—never take this gift for granted. So today, remember the important role that friendship plays in your marriage. That friendship is, after all, a glorious gift, praised by God. Give thanks for that gift and nurture it.

A TIP

Your choice of friends is critically important.
If you want to accomplish your hightest aspirations,
you should choose friends who will encourage
you to accomplish those aspirations.

---

*A friend loves you all the time,
and a brother helps in time of trouble.*

Proverbs 17:17 NCV

Promises from God's Word About . . .
FRIENDSHIP AND LOVE

Beloved, if God so loved us,
we also ought to love one another.

1 John 4:11 NKJV

I thank my God upon every remembrance of you.

Philippians 1:3 NKJV

A friend loves at all times,
and a brother is born for adversity.

Proverbs 17:17 NIV

Iron sharpeneth iron; so a man sharpeneth
the countenance of his friend.

Proverbs 27:17 KJV

More Ideas About . . .
FRIENDSHIP AND LOVE

True friends don't spend time gazing into each
other's eyes. They show great tenderness toward
each other, but they face in the same direction,
toward common projects, interest, goals,
and above all, toward a common Lord.

C. S. Lewis

God has not called us to see through each other,
but to see each other through.

Jess Moody

You can make more friends in two months by
becoming more interested in other people
than you can in two years by trying to get
other people interested in you.

Dale Carnegie

Friendship is the garden of God;
what a delight to tend his planting!

Inez Bell Ley

Promises from God's Word About . . .
FRIENDSHIP AND LOVE

Greater love has no one than this,
that he lay down his life for his friends.

John 15:13 NIV

If a fellow believer hurts you, go and tell him—
work it out between the two of you.
If he listens, you've made a friend.

Matthew 18:15 MSG

Beloved, if God so loved us,
we also ought to love one another.

1 John 4:11 NKJV

Finally, all of you be of one mind,
having compassion for one another; love as brothers,
be tenderhearted, be courteous.

1 Peter 3:8 NKJV

More Ideas About . . .
FRIENDSHIP AND LOVE

I have found that the closer I am to the godly people
around me, the easier it is for me to live a righteous
life because they hold me accountable.

John MacArthur

The best times in life are made a thousand times
better when shared with a dear friend.

Luci Swindoll

We are indeed rich when we have many friends,
and I am thoroughly convinced that God loves us,
encourages us, nurtures us, and supports us
through other human beings.

Marilyn Meberg

Old friends are a comfort to the heart.
Like a favorite robe and a familiar song,
they wrap you in the warmth of their presence and
you understand all the words.

Pat Matuszak

A TIP

If you're trying to make new friends,
become interested in them . . .
and eventually they'll become interested in you.

A PRAYER

Dear Lord, I thank You for the joys of friendship.
You have brought wonderful Christian friends into
my life. Let me enrich their lives in the same way
that they have enriched mine. And let us all glorify
You as we follow in the footsteps of Your Son.
Amen

ALLOW CHRIST TO REIGN

At the name of Jesus every knee should bow, of those in heaven, and of those on earth, and of those under the earth, and that every tongue should confess that Jesus Christ is Lord, to the glory of God the Father.

Philippians 2:10-11 NKJV

A Christ-centered marriage is an exercise in faith, love, fidelity, trust, understanding, forgiveness, caring, sharing, and encouragement. It requires empathy, tenderness, patience, and perseverance. It is the union of two Christian adults, both of whom are willing to compromise and, when appropriate, to apologize. A Christ-centered marriage requires heaping helpings of common sense, common courtesy, and uncommon caring. It is a joy to behold, a joy to experience, and a blessing forever.

Does Christ truly preside over your marriage, or does He occupy a position of lesser importance? The answer to that question will determine the quality and direction of your marriage. When both you and your spouse allow Jesus to reign over your lives, Christ will bless you and your family in wonderful, unexpected ways. So today and every day, make your marriage a model of Christian love, respect, and service. Jesus expects no less, and neither, for that matter, should you.

A TIP

Let Jesus make a real difference in your life:
If you're trying to mold your relationship with
Jesus into something that fits comfortably into your
own schedule and your own personal theology, you
may be headed for trouble. A far better strategy is
this: conform yourself to Jesus, not vice versa.

*Jesus Christ the same yesterday,
and today, and for ever.*

Hebrews 13:8 KJV

Promises from God's Word About . . .
JESUS

In the beginning was the Word, and the Word was with God, and the Word was God.... And the Word was made flesh, and dwelt among us, (and we beheld his glory, the glory as of the only begotten of the Father,) full of grace and truth.

John 1:1, 14 KJV

For Jesus is the one referred to in the Scriptures, where it says, 'The stone that you builders rejected has now become the cornerstone.' There is salvation in no one else! There is no other name in all of heaven for people to call on to save them."

Acts 4:11-12 NLT

I am the Vine, you are the branches. When you're joined with me and I with you, the relation intimate and organic, the harvest is sure to be abundant.

John 15:5 MSG

More Ideas About . . .
JESUS

Jesus was the Savior Who would deliver them
not only from the bondage of sin but also from
meaningless wandering through life.

Anne Graham Lotz

Jesus is the personal approach from the unseen God
coming so near that he becomes inescapable.
You don't have to find him—you just have
to consent to be found.

E. Stanley Jones

There is not a single thing that Jesus cannot change,
control, and conquer because He is the living Lord.

Franklin Graham

The Word had become flesh, a real human baby. He
had not ceased to be God. He was no less God then
than before, but He had begun to be man. He was
not now God minus some elements of His deity but
God plus all that He had made His own by taking
manhood to himself.

J. I. Packer

Promises from God's Word About . . .
LOVING JESUS

*The next day John saw Jesus coming toward him
and said, "Here is the Lamb of God,
who takes away the sin of the world!*

John 1:29 Holman CSB

*But we do see Jesus—made lower than the angels for a
short time so that by God's grace He might taste death
for everyone—crowned with glory and honor
because of the suffering of death.*

Hebrews 2:9 Holman CSB

I am the door. If anyone enters by Me, he will be saved.

John 10:9 NKJV

*I am the true vine, and My Father is the vineyard
keeper. Every branch in Me that does not produce fruit
He removes, and He prunes every branch that produces
fruit so that it will produce more fruit.*

John 15:1-2 Holman CSB

More Ideas About . . .
LOVING JESUS

In His humanness, Jesus was a victim, mercilessly hammered to a cross after being spat upon, mocked, and humiliated. But in His deity, He promised the thief on the cross eternal life, as only God can.

John MacArthur

Christians see sin for what it is: willful rebellion against the rulership of God in their lives. And in turning from their sin, they have embraced God's only means of dealing with sin: Jesus.

Kay Arthur

In your greatest weakness, turn to your greatest strength, Jesus, and hear Him say, "My grace is sufficient for you, for My strength is made perfect in weakness"(2 Corinthians 12:9, NKJV).

Lisa Whelchel

Heavenly forcast: Jesus will REIGN forever!

Anonymous

A TIP

What a friend you have in Jesus: Jesus loves you,
and He offers you eternal life with Him in heaven.
Welcome Him into your heart. Now!

A PRAYER

Lord, You sent Your Son so that I might have
a life that is abundant and eternal.
Thank You, Lord, for Jesus, for His sacrifices,
and for His love. Because Jesus is my Savior,
I am blessed by His grace forever.
Amen

What therefore God hath joined together,
let not man put asunder.

Matthew 19:6 KJV

Marriage should be honored by everyone,
and husband and wife
should keep their marriage pure.

Let love and faithfulness
never leave you . . .
write them on the tablet of your heart.

Proverbs 3:3 NIV